Sales H
of Winners

Master the fundamentals of B2B sales with easy to understand checklists

Jan Ropponen

Contact publisher:
www.axend.fi
jan.ropponen@axend.fi
+358 50 5169392

ISBN 978-952-69079-3-2 (paperback)
ISBN 978-952-69079-4-9 (EPUB)

Table of Contents

Introduction

What unites Olympic athletes, top surgeons and the best pilots in the world?

These high-performers have all developed exceptional attention to detail, learned (and earned!) through consistent routine. When combining this with an unparalleled passion for one's professional pursuits, you have a recipe for success.

The world's biggest and best victories are only possible through consistent routine and practice. Over time, consistency equates to dependability. Forgetting to follow consistent routines or procedures can even lead to tragedy in some professions. When someone has an optimum skill set, if those skills are not applied consistently, success will be elusive.

Sales professionals are not always known for their consistent work styles, and while many sales professionals perform well, their inconsistency in behavior can sometimes be reflected in their overall annual performance. Some successful, more experienced sales people tend to rely on the habits and intuition they have developed over their long careers. They do very well for themselves, even though sometimes these experienced salespeople cannot even themselves explain exactly what they are doing to achieve results.

Succeeding in sales is however getting tougher all the time and not everyone has the luxury of decades of experience. The environment we now work in as sales professionals is highly global, digital and hyper-fast. Customers have more options that ever before and they view vendors in many industries more and more as commodities because they cannot necessarily differentiate between vendors. As a result, working as a sales professional has forever changed and will keep changing. It's not going to get any easier from here either.

We need to sell smarter than ever before, continuously working to add value to customers. It's just not enough that you have better products and services than your competitors. Though superior products and services are extremely important in today's sales' climate, you still need more of an edge to insure success. As sales professionals, we must now increase our brain-work without decreasing our leg-work. This means we must choose which prospects (and therefore, which opportunities) to pursue much more carefully, putting a higher quality of effort into those opportunities that we do choose to pursue, as opposed to reaching out to any and all prospects by committing to the pursuit of all opportunities. This doesn't mean we visit customers less; it just means we need to focus our efforts much more than ever before. We need to outsmart *and* outwork our competitors.

The quality of the basics of our work has become more important for those sales professionals who want to perform consistently and become leaders in the field. It's these basics that are the core of this book and they've been summarized through easy-to-use checklists.

Who Is This Book For?

This book is an especially good fit for those working on deals between $5k-$100k. It doesn't matter which industry you work in as long as your work involves talking to customers. Whether face-to-face or remotely, this book is for you.

For some, the checklists and story in this book may be a transformational experience that boosts careers to a whole new level. I've also received positive feedback on the practicality of the checklists found in this book from experienced sales professionals winning deals between $100k-$500k. Whether you are a typical account executive, in sales development, a sales representative role, or, you do sales here and there as a consultant, these checklists will help you succeed. Your customers will be happier when you use the checklist method and you'll earn more commissions and bonuses–win-win!

Here are some topics that the checklists will give guidance on:

- Prospecting & booking meetings
- Running meetings & discovering the customer's challenges
- Building proposals
- Presenting and working on proposals with the customer
- Negotiating & winning deals

"No wise pilot, no matter how great his talent and experience, fails to use his checklist"
-Charlie Munger

The Power of Checklists

Perhaps the most well-known professionals who use checklists are airline pilots. The airline industry isn't the only field that has been positively impacted by checklists; professions such as medicine, manufacturing, consulting, or any professional service organizations benefit as well. While every business can benefit from the use of checklists, when it comes to sales, many in the field prefer to "wing it" by trusting their instincts. Checklists and routines are what differentiate professionals from amateurs, whether you're a pilot, a health care professional, a consultant, or, in sales.

The goal of a sales-checklist is to enable sales professionals to consistently stay at peak-performance levels. Checklists are important because human psychology is not designed to deal with the complexity of a typical B2B sales process. As a sales person, you are often simultaneously working on multiple deals with multiple prospects, while also engaging with more than one stakeholder. It's easy to skip certain steps or simply forget to include details necessary to make the sale. Not only are B2B deals complex, it can also be very stressful process. You are constantly monitored and expected to make your quota. When you work under pressure, it's a relief to have a process to fall back on to insure everything will be covered. There are hundreds of minor details impacting the probability of failure, as well as success. By using the checklists in this book, you will become a top performer, and perhaps more importantly, stay a top performer.

Best Practices of Selling are Universal

Some deals can be more straightforward than others, requiring only one or two meetings to close, whereas more complex sales can mean anywhere between 5-20 meetings. The checklists will help you in every sales situation. That's why these lists are not only for sales professionals that sell everyday but they can also be used by experts in professional services that sell occasionally when not doing billable work.

There are many paths and ways to succeed in sales; the checklists are not absolute rules. Consider each checklist a guideline of universal best practices. By applying the practices in the checklists, you should accelerate your deal cycles, as well as improve the quality of the opportunities you are working on.

The Structure of the Book

The checklists presented in this book are a compilation of best practices personally acquired through thousands of new business meetings and training many hundreds of sales people, as well as ideas collected in my own notes from the past decade of training and applied research. It can be shocking sometimes to see how even the most experienced sales professionals working on larger opportunities will take short-cuts or forget to do things that are critical to win the sale. It's for this reason that these checklists have been created. I've noticed that using checklists, even if only for a little while, can create profitable habits that lead to a lifetime of success.

I have probably made all the mistakes we're covering in this book more than once. Over time, I've found a way to get the fundamentals right, but I didn't learn them all at the same time. First, it was about mastering how to get meetings. Then, I noticed my meetings weren't resulting in good enough outcomes. Once I made some adjustments and meetings were going well, I focused on improving proposals. One step at a time and thousands of meetings and proposals later, each part of the process is finally going smoothly from end-to-end.

In *Sales Habits of Winners*, each chapter starts by presenting some typical challenges salespeople usually face. This is a good place to stop and reflect if you also experience the same types of challenges in your work. After this you will be brought on a journey to follow a fictional story and character to follow. At the end of each chapter, there will be checklist to help you with that specific part of your work that has been covered in the chapter. Here are the five sections of the book, which will each have at least one checklist.

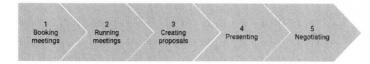

The checklists were initially designed for someone that hunts for new customers, but they work just as well for an account manager working with specific accounts, as he/she needs to consistently discover new opportunities, create proposals and negotiate. Whether you spend time acquiring new customers or selling to existing customers, these checklists will be useful for you.

You'll notice that the checklists and the amount of content is more robust in the first half of the book and there is a good reason for that. The further along in the sales process you go, the less options you have for impacting the probability that the customer will buy. When you are presenting a proposal and heading into the negotiating stage, much of the critical sales work should have been done already.

You will also notice that some parts of the checklists are more direct, while others are presented as questions. Some things are simpler, than others to do, so those are presented directly as things to do in the checklists. The things that require more thinking that change depending on the situation you are in are presented as broader questions in the checklists.

Welcome, Daniel!

"Daniel" is a fictional sales professional and the "hero" of our "story." Instead of just providing a series of checklists, it will be easier to grasp the concepts presented in the book by following the story of Daniel as he works on an opportunity and moves through the different stages of the sales process. It's important to note that our "story" represents real-life challenges and situations that have actually happened. The companies and names have all been changed.

Daniel is a 38-year-old sales professional. He started his sales career when he was 26. Daniel works for an accounting and financial services firm called Ross Finance and Accounting (RFA).

RFA offers financial and accounting help in the form of an outsourced CFO, as well as accounting services. Typically, an outsourced CFO costs between $10k - $100k annually; normal accounting can be between $5k-$200k, depending on the size of the business. Daniel has always been a top-performer in the company; he is one of 50 account managers spread nationally across the different offices of RFA. Daniel has not always been the most systematic sales person, but when he really focuses on a specific opportunity, he has had good results.

The story starts in August as Daniel has just received the news that a large customer will be switching over to another provider of the same services Daniel offers. To hit his target next year, which will be higher than this year, Daniel will need to find at least 2-3 new mid-sized customers, as well as expand on his current customers.

We will follow Daniel's journey as he works on finding (and landing!) one new prospect account. He will be navigating through some challenges, and at the end of every chapter, you can use the checklists to see how he did. The words used to describe the customer are mainly "prospect" in chapter one and "buyer" or "customer" in chapter two. We switch over to using the term "customer," as it applies to working with both existing and new potential customers.

If you are interested in using Daniel's templates and tools, as well as getting additional guidance, you can visit courses.janropponen.com

Buckle up and get ready for a fun, fast (and sometimes bumpy!) ride as "Daniel

Masters" shows us how to navigate towards finding and winning over a new customer.

I really hope you enjoy the book, and more importantly, can use it to become more successful!

-Jan Ropponen

PS: I'd love your feedback and comments about the book on social media (#saleshabits). Even better, if you enjoy the book, please write a review on Amazon.

Chapter 1: Booking a Meeting

Typical Challenges When Booking a Meeting

Cold outreach doesn't work well in today's sales climate. Prospects do not answer phones like they used to. It can also be difficult to reach decision-makers via other channels. Prospects have become highly independent and confident in their ability to do research on their own when the time is right for them, instead of relying on sales reps for information.

Knowing who to contact is tough. Complex organizations and special titles make it harder to know who to contact. In addition to this, it's not easy to define which types of prospect companies would be the best to focus on.

Prospecting done right is time consuming. Highly customized and relevant messages work for booking meetings. But creating those messages takes a lot of time. When done right, prospecting can be time consuming if you don't know how to focus your efforts.

Deciding Who to Target

It's August 10th. Daniel has started working on figuring out which companies would be the best potential new customers for him. He doesn't need to start from scratch because he has been networking with many companies in the last few years. He decides to create a short-list based on the prospects and contacts he already knows personally. Daniel's short-list includes the top twenty prospects with the most potential. When evaluating potential prospects, Daniel takes into account the prospect's maturity, market and industry; he then aligns those factors with the strengths and references of RFA.

Daniel knows the happiest customers with RFA are in manufacturing and IT—both are considered growth industries. He also has a good feel for the typical size a prospect company should be both from an employee and revenue perspective. RFA clients tend to generate revenue between $3-million and $100-million and have a range of 20-300 employees. Smaller companies looking to grow are more interesting to RFA, as opposed to large, stable businesses. RFA can help with outsourced CFO services and scale up the service level as needed, which leaves little room for risk in recruiting for the customer.

Based on this, Daniel decides to focus on manufacturing companies that seem to be in a growing market, or, that have a growth strategy.

> *"At least 50% of the prospects sales people contact are not a good fit for what they sell"*[1]

Finding a Suitable Approach

It's August 16th. Daniel looks for information and prepares to contact the companies on his shortlist, but there is one particular company that sticks out from the beginning: PB Corporation. Daniel contacted the company's CEO the year before but had no luck getting a meeting. PB Corporation is a manufacturer of traditional plastic products such as buckets, containers, cups, and so forth. They had a partner the last time Daniel was in touch with them. Now that Daniel is taking another look, he notices that their situation has changed. Based on an article Daniel found, PB Corporation is looking to expand their business; they have recently hired a new CEO as well. PB Corporation has been a family business, and for the first time in the company's history, they have hired a CEO outside of the family.

PB Corporation is not a public company, so it's not easy to find company information. But with a bit of digging (Google, etc.), Daniel finds the information he needs. An article in an industry publication called *PlastiTech Magazine* features an interview with PB Corp's owner and the newly-appointed CEO. The article talks about PB Corporation's intentions to expand into bio-plastics, which would mean building a new production line, as well as expanding their factory. The article is not clear as to when or how the new product line will be launched; the focus of the article was about where the global markets are heading and what the trends in the plastics business are. When asked if this new focus could risk or cannibalize their old highly profitable business, the CEO stated that PB Corporation was headed into a new growth phase, so profit was not their primary concern.

Through further research Daniel notices that PB Corporation has recently acquired a small bio-plastics company, which fits with the story in the magazine.

Daniel also reads press releases and skims through a few annual reports of publicly-traded companies in the same industry to get hints at what the pain-points and potential development areas are for these companies.

Based on RFA's strengths, and the references PB Corporation made in the article, it makes sense that this could be a company that fits into what Daniel can offer if they are looking to expand the business, which was not a priority the last time Daniel spoke with the CEO of the company.

Daniel knows he needs to find a winning angle in order to get the meeting. "A winning angle" is something Daniel refers to when he can get in touch with prospects, and no matter what their objection is, he can schedule a meeting. The best way to do this is to find a common acquaintance that Daniel can mention, but he doesn't have any social connections with PB Corp, so he will have to make sure his approach is irrefutable.

"You are 4.2x more likely to get an appointment if you have a personal connection with a buyer "[2]

Contacting the Prospects

It's August 19th. Daniel decides to use the article in *PlastiTech Magazine* as support for his approach. He builds his messaging around the typical challenges for growth that traditional manufacturing companies have, and, what capturing this growth opportunity would entail.

Daniel has problems getting a hold of the new CEO at PB Corporation. Last time he spoke with the former CEO of PB Corporation, he had an easy time getting in touch. Now with this new CEO, the situation is quite the opposite. Daniel has called several times and sent many emails without a response. Here is one of the last emails he sent:

Hi, Anders,

Tried to get a hold of you today in the afternoon via phone. I noticed the article in PlastiTech Magazine *about your new investments and growth opportunity in bio-plastics.*

Launching new technology and entering new markets, like many of our clients do, may bring unforeseen challenges that impact your cash flow. I'd like to share some insights with you about our customers and how we helped them to succeed in their growth plans. What would it take to get 5-10 minutes of time over the phone, say, tomorrow afternoon?

Looking forward to talking to you--

Best regards,

Daniel

Daniel has trouble getting a response and notices from his email tracking application that Anders has not even opened his email. Daniel switches the subject line on the email, making the email much shorter. On his third email, he gets a response from the CEO. It's now the 22nd of August:

"Sure, let's have a quick chat. Call me 5 PM tomorrow"

> ## *"Only 24% of sales emails are opened"*[3]

Daniel knows from his experience that short, smartphone-readable messages work; if the message is brief, valuable, and has a meaningful context to the company's overall business, and it has a clear call to action.

Daniel calls at 5 PM and the prospect, Anders, picks up.

Anders, the new CEO, immediately sounds skeptical on the phone, saying they already have a good relationship with their current accounting firm.

Daniel: *"Yes, that is exactly why I called you. The article I read was about your growth goals, and your new acquisition tells me that you are getting ready for a new critical phase in the company's history. Have I evaluated your situation correctly?"*

Anders: *"Well, yes, we do plan on growing."*

Daniel goes on to explain: *"Our focus is on helping customers grow, not doing accounting based on what has already happened, but instead making sure you have no barriers to achieving growth by improving sales-forecasting and production-cost planning. Almost all our customers have growth plans that don't go exactly the way they expected. That's where we can help."*

Daniel asks a question about their financial planning, they talk for a moment and then Daniel suggests:

"If we setup up a meeting, I can show you a few example cases of our customers who are also in the manufacturing business and show you how they solved their challenges while growing rapidly...how would that sound?"

Anders doesn't say, "yes," or, "no." but is open to discussing it a bit more. During the phone call, Daniel and Anders have a 10-minute discussion about the business in general and why Anders decided to join PB Corporation from his previous CEO role at another manufacturing company. This additional information gives Daniel a good understanding of where PB Corporation stands and what the first meeting's agenda should be.

What Daniel doesn't know at this point is that, while Anders is happy with the current accounting firm, the COO has been raising her concerns about how the current accountants are going to handle growth as PB Corporation launches the new product line. The current accounting firm is just doing basic accounting, without giving PB Corporation solid advice about how they should develop the business. PB Corporation does have a finance manager, but he has been around more to create reports for management and managing the accounting firm itself. The COO has also made the observation that PB Corporation's current ERP system may be outdated. Daniel knows RFA can resolve all of these concerns and more. He just has to sell the solution to key stakeholders like Anders and Amanda at PB Corporation.

Deciding Next Steps

Anders still doesn't want to meet, but he does ask Daniel to setup up a call with their COO, Amanda.

After the call, Daniel sends a thank you email to the CEO, and CC's the COO, Amanda. He writes a brief summary:

Hi Anders,
cc: Amanda

Thanks for the discussion about your growth ambitions. As discussed, I'll get in touch with Amanda to see her points of view and see if she would be interested in walking through how some manufacturers that consider themselves to be growth companies have navigated successfully through their growth phases from a financial perspective.

Best regards,

Daniel

It's August 25th. Daniel gets in touch with the COO, Amanda, the next morning and is able to book the meeting. Amanda also seems a bit skeptical but is open to look at what Daniel can show about the other manufacturing companies. Amanda typically accepts "cold" meeting proposals only if she thinks the sales person can explain something about competitors or give her new ideas. She doesn't have time to go to seminars, so she likes using quick meetings as a way to keep herself up to date with what is going on in the market place regarding new solutions and technology.

Prospecting Checklists

Tasks	Yes	No
Prospects on your target list are a good fit or, preferably, "sweet-spot" customers for the products and services you provide		
You have identified what your strong references are that can be used when booking meetings		
You have identified what types of results you have achieved for similar customers before contacting the prospect		
You have checked if you have mutual contacts with the prospect on LinkedIn or connections in other social channels you can leverage		
You understand the changes and trends going on in the prospect's industry right now and how they impact the prospect's business		
You have information about changes going on within the prospect's company (these changes can be organizational changes, new products etc. which can act as triggers that open up a window of opportunity for new vendors and solutions)		
You have a plan or routine for using multiple different touches in various channels (email, phone, LinkedIn, SMS, voicemail etc.)		
You know your strengths and weaknesses versus your various competitors		
You have a compelling message and can leverage your unique value proposition in such a way that it will make it difficult to reject a meeting proposal		
If none of the above get you a meeting with your dream prospect, you have a way to follow the prospect and their business until a		

suitable event happens that will trigger them to want to meet with you		

Phone Checklist

Tasks	Yes	No
When calling, optimize your time and efforts. Typically, mornings (8-9) and end of the workday (4-5) produce better results		
You can clearly and easily define what the tangible benefits are to the prospect for meeting with you for one hour		
Get the prospect engaged right away on the phone with a calm and powerful start		
Open the phone call with a relevant question or value statement followed by a relevant question		
Explain how the prospect benefits from meeting with you		
Utilize multiple channels for support: Social media, email, SMS, voicemail		
Handle objections intuitively & listen to understand a prospect's concerns better		
Drive for a next step aggressively, but in a highly professional manner		
If the prospect requests a new time to be contacted, propose a time and agenda. Best practice is to send them an invite so that you are fully aligned		

Chapter 2: Running a Meeting

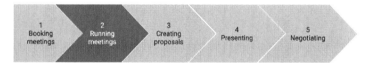

Typical Challenges When Running Sales Meetings

Weak preparation: Simple things that prepare the buyer and the sales person for the meeting are not done, such as sending an agenda to all the meeting attendees.

Weak opening of the meeting: Especially when meeting new prospects, the prospect does not trust the sales person. Even small things that are unclear can annoy and make the prospect seem unsure or uncomfortable. In the beginning of the meeting, the goal and agenda are not always clear to the prospect, and the sales person doesn't properly authorize themselves as a subject-matter expert. This leads to a situation where the prospect doesn't trust the sales person or see how answering the sales person's questions will give them any value in return, so they hesitate to share a lot of important information during the meeting.

Poor discovery and questioning: Discussions wander off-topic or sporadically from one topic to the next without logic. Often the sales person is not prepared to discuss about the prospect's business, and it shows immediately. When the sales person does uncover relevant information, he/she often forgets to confirm that he/she has understood things correctly.

Poor qualification before deciding how to move forward: Prospects are almost always interested in seeing a proposal, but that doesn't mean they want to even consider buying. Many sales people start preparing proposals after an initial meeting without qualifying if they prospect is truly interested in buying.

Unclear next steps and gaining commitment: Many meetings end without clear consensus on what the next steps should be; the buyer is clearly not committed to investing any of their time to evaluating the solution and its implications, but a salesperson still sends a proposal. It's also not uncommon to forget to send a memo of the meeting, which includes clear next-steps.

Starting the Meeting

It's September 18th. Daniel starts the meeting by walking through the agenda and goals. While going through the agenda, Daniel asks Amanda if it's okay that he presents some questions about their goals and strategy so he can make sure the cases he's presenting are aligned with the right business challenges.

> *"Only 3% of buyers trust reps. The only professions with less credibility include car sales, politics and lobbying."*[4]

Amanda answers with a short few words along the lines of, "Of course, that's fine."

After an introduction round and discussion of both Amanda's and Daniel's backgrounds, as well as some small-talk, Daniel gives a very brief three-minute presentation about the references of RFA and the results they have achieved for their clients. As they walk through the references, Daniel shares how he has also personally been involved with customers and which industries and problems he has been solving while working as an account manager at RFA. Within a few short minutes, Daniel knows he either has or doesn't have the trust of the prospect. He also knows that how the beginning of the meeting goes dictates how open the customer is throughout the whole meeting.

In the beginning of the meeting, Amanda already makes it clear that they are very happy with their current accounting partner.

Daniel knew this already, but he sensed something was off when he contacted the CEO; they just weren't telling him yet what it was that they would need help with.

Understanding the Buyer's Situation

> ### *"82% of B2B decision-makers think sales reps are unprepared"*[5]

After the introductions, and two slides about RFA, Daniel switches over to the next slide titled: "Typical Growth Challenges for Manufacturers." Although Daniel already has permission to ask about PB Corporation's goals and strategy, he prefers to lead the discussion towards the prospect's situation, by first looking at how other companies are working. This is the approach he uses to earn the right to ask more difficult questions to get more in-depth information about the buyer's business, including their challenges and pain-points.

> ## *"Roughly 58% of buyers say their sales meetings aren't valuable."*[6]

Amanda agrees with many of the points on the slide, and bit by bit, she becomes more talkative. This is a natural point in the discussion to switch over the focus to PB Corporation. Daniel brings in the topic of PB Corporation's acquisition and mentions that their CEO, Anders, said this could be their hope for growth in the future, as traditional product-sales are declining. Daniel asks Amanda if the growth goals are really as ambitious as their CEO portrayed in the magazine interview.

After a long discussion about the market and the high-level strategy of PB Corporation, Daniel points out what the role of RFA has been with the clients who are expanding their businesses. Daniel decides to play it safe and stick with a discussion about what the different needs are when comparing a stable business and a growth business, and what the role of a CFO is in each of these.

It turns out that Amanda had understood the value proposition of RFA a bit wrong. She thought they were just an accounting firm, but now realizes that the challenges Daniel is outlining are exactly the same challenges PB Corporation is facing, and now, she realizes things will only get worse as they begin executing their new strategy.

Amanda is ready to reveal her true challenges and the headache she sees coming via PB Corporation's growth strategy. It turns out that the family that owns the company wants profitability levels to remain high, while also pushing for growth. They have invested a lot of money in building the new production line and the acquisition itself, but they haven't prepared to invest in developing new business processes, systems and procedures. There is no pain yet, but

Amanda reveals that it has been difficult to plan for the growth phase with the current accounting firm, and their in-house finance manager hasn't had experience with similar situations. Additionally, she explains to Daniel that she is not so sure they even have the right resource planning and finance software at the moment, but the finance manager thinks they do.

Probing for Pain and Implications

Daniel knows that Amanda is experiencing some discomfort, but he is sure that if her discomfort does not turn into pain, then there will be no incentive for Amanda to want to take RFA on as a partner as it would mean making some changes and more cost. The time needed of bringing a new partner up to speed would take her focus away from other important things. She would have to convince the CEO, the finance manager, and the owners that change is needed. Amanda is very new with the company as she just started in August, so she seems like she wants to carefully think about which of her ideas to bring to the CEO.

Daniel has seen this before: The prospect knows that their current set-up is not optimal and is causing problems, but the problems are not necessarily serious enough that the situation would warrant the prospect to have to change. These prospects end up focusing on things that have a larger impact on the business, postponing the decision. Daniel needs to understand more about PB Corporation so that he can consult and help them see their situation from a new angle and then help them see what their best options are. This type of consultative work already happens in this first meeting and it continues through the whole sales process.

The company is family owned, but the management is not family. The father who founded the company retired a few years ago. Daniel now understands that the family wants the business to remain profitable but also capture the growth opportunity, which Daniel knows is extremely difficult. Typically, either profit or growth is focused on at any one time—not both.

Daniel guides Amanda with a series of questions so she understands the risk of pursuing their ambitious targets with the current partner they have. They will need to hire lots of engineers, factory workers and invest in sales & marketing. They must spend their money wisely as they steer the business towards a growth path. Cash flow will be very tight, and it must be monitored closely. Throughout the discussion, it becomes clearer to Daniel that PB Corporation's IT-systems are, in fact, not optimal. But at this point, it might be a long-shot to start changing them.

Challenging the Customer if Necessary

During the meeting Daniel asks questions like:

"Do you think your current finance manager will actively be able to forecast and assist you in navigating through this?"

It turns out that the current finance manager has a very administrative role. He has been a finance manager in the family business for over 20 years and is a close family friend. The finance manager does not have the background nor any experience in strategic finance. The finance manager reports directly to Amanda, but she explains that they are having a hard time speaking the same language and have differing opinions on strategic matters, such as forecasting or even creating reports that are easier for the management team to understand. Amanda is a bit worried about the current finance manager and his competencies in the new areas where expertise is sorely needed.

Daniel also uncovers information in the meeting about the newly acquired bioplastic research company which has very recently made a break-through in their research and development. Starting next year, PB Corporation will be looking to double their sales if they are able to ramp up production and build the right sales channels. The goal is to be fully operational at the end of this year, and then start shipping the new products in January of the following year.

In addition to finding new sales channels, PB Corporation has decided they will also test out how they would be able to sell directly to consumers globally. Traditionally PB Corporation has only sold their products through traditional retail channels and wholesalers. They will keep doing that as well, but also open up web-shops for new markets.

Amanda and Daniel discuss how this will add complexity to the business and its forecasting. Since the owners want to see a steady profit yet are still pushing for PB Corporation to ambitiously go after growth targets, it will be crucial to align production and sales to avoid buying too much raw material and producing goods that will take up valuable inventory space. PB Corporation must succeed at aligning market demand and their production. And, RFA can help. That's Daniel's in.

Sales and marketing initiatives are already starting in the fall of this year to create demand in the market. Amanda says to Daniel:

"Based on what we've talked about, it would be interesting to see what this outsourced CFO service could help us with as we launch the new business line, but we want to keep our current accounting firm"

Daniel knows this may be a problem, because if they start with a CFO service, the synergies are very high with having the basic accounting service as well. Daniel needs to get the basic accounting and CFO service in use at the same time to get the best value out of their partnership with clients. Daniel also senses at this point that, Peter, the finance manager, will most likely be concerned about job security when topics like this are discussed.

Towards the end of the meeting, Amanda asks, *"So, how much does the outsourced CFO service typically cost?"* Daniel doesn't share price information at this point because he knows he is a provider of a premium service that some customers are not used to buying; it requires careful positioning for the customer to entirely understand the value. Daniel has learned that introducing pricing too early can result in a situation where the customer will not be able to understand the value his firm can provide if fixated on the price. The cost is not directly comparable to other service providers with a lower quality of service, so Daniel must first build in the context of the service, as well as the benefits it provides to customers like PB Corporation. Price is just a number, but conveying the value of a service or product can be quite complex.

> ## *"Nearly 6/10 buyers want to discuss pricing on the first call"[7]*

Daniel redirects the discussion from price to PB Corporation's goals, saying that cost depends on a number of factors and he'd need to go over what those factors may be in more detail with one of RFA's expert CFOs. Daniel also explains that one big question is their IT systems, which they will have to have a closer look at before giving a price indication.

Qualifying Before Proceeding

Daniel decides (out of habit) to do a light qualification before deciding on whether to move forward with PB Corporation. He wants to get a better understanding of whether or not he actually has a good chance at getting a deal out of this, as well as what the potential timeframe would be.

> *"Buyers are less concerned with the qualifying topics salespeople are usually most interested in: Just one in four want to discuss budget, authority, and timeline."*[8]

Daniel has learned that if the first meeting goes well, then the customer most certainly always wants to meet again. This is free consulting for the client, so there is also always the risk for good sales people that are able to consult with the customer, that the customer doesn't actually want to buy but instead wants to meet to reap the most value from each meeting. Daniel has noticed that if many people are invited to meetings, they are often brought along for educational purposes. They may even have a notebook and take notes during the meeting although they have nothing to do with making decisions or sometimes not even close to being influencers that impact the buying decision. This is usually a clear case of free consultation/training for the client.

Before suggesting next steps, Daniel proceeds with his light qualification to understand better the customer's true agenda. Additionally, Daniel wants to have a rough timeline and a grasp on how decisions are typically made at PB Corporation. Daniel doesn't just qualify once like some sales people do, because he sees qualification as being something that happens in every meeting and call. Each time he interacts with the prospect, his picture improves of how qualified the opportunity is.

The following topics are discussed:

Need: There is a definite need, but Daniel sees it is not yet a critical need, as the problems haven't hit them. Amanda brings up the fact that she thinks they could also buy the service from their current accounting partner, this makes Daniel think that he needs to take this into account down the road as they move forward. He's learned that if he knows about the customers options, then it's much easier for him to position RFA and their solution to win.

Timeline: Since production should be ramped up in Q1 of next year, RFA would need to start the service in November or December to minimize risks of starting too late.

> **"In a typical firm with 100-500 employees, an average of 7 people are involved in most buying decisions."** [2]

Decision-making: To figure this out Daniel asks, *"If we were to move forward together, how do you typically decide on something like this at PB Corporation?"* Daniel needs to understand both the formal and informal ways of making decisions in the company. Amanda says that first they need a management meeting and after that, if everything looks good, they can proceed.

Budget: As far as Amanda knows, PB Corporation was not planning on budgeting for this type of service within the next year. Daniel has learned to do qualification from a few different angles at the end of each sales meeting, because so many of his deals have ended up as so called "dry runs." This is a situation where the customer says they need something and are looking to purchase, but in the end, the customer never actually makes a final decision, remaining with the current solution or deciding they don't need to buy anything after all.

With so many question marks and hurdles to climb over at this point, Daniel will need to do a very good job of selling to be able to get a decision by the end of the year.

Gaining Commitment for Next Steps

At the end of this meeting, Amanda requests that a proposal be sent to her so she can share it with Anders, the CEO. Daniel says that he doesn't quite have a full picture yet but has enough information to create a draft of a proposal that they can go through together face-to-face. He tells Amanda he will not be sending it, as there are too many points that need to be discussed together in person, as well as many other variables that impact the potential results that may be achieved together.

Daniel explains that he now has enough information that it would make sense to bring along a senior CFO from RFA to the next meeting to go through a presentation of their findings. The tradeoff Daniel proposes is that Daniel will bring the experienced CFO along with him if PB Corporation's CEO, Anders, also comes to the meeting. Daniel concludes by offering:

"Anders can come in and listen to an executive summary and a reference case, and then leave the meeting if he wishes to do so."

Daniel and Amanda agree that this is a fair way to move forward; Amanda suggests that they should also bring the finance manager, Peter. Understanding what Daniel now understands, he suggests that the meeting should just include Amanda and Anders.

Daniel hopes this will be an easier route towards an agreement if he can get Anders to participate in the next meeting. If Daniel can have both Amanda and Anders in the same room, he can then discuss some of the key points between them during the meeting. Otherwise, it may be a rocky road as Amanda will have to sell this idea on her own in separate discussions to Anders, without Daniel being able to participate and influence the discussion.

Even though Amanda agrees to leaving Peter out of the next meeting, she has second thoughts about bringing Anders in. They decide she will discuss this with Anders before deciding on next-steps. Daniel knows most prospects are interested in seeing proposals after the first meeting, but only some are ready to make a commitment by investing their time. In Daniel's experience, the prospects that are willing to spend time are more serious and more likely to buy. It also depends on what level and position the person is in. Sometimes Daniel has noticed that some very operative personnel are willing to spend as much time with Daniel as he is willing to spend with them, but it doesn't lead to anything because they have no direct decision-making power or enough influence within the organization.

Amanda cannot be sure if she can get Anders to join, so Daniel suggests she discuss it with Anders. Amanda and Daniel set-up a call in two days. Overall, the meeting is positive because Daniel noticed a change in Amanda's attitude and it is clear that there is a need, as well as a certain level of pain being experienced at the moment.

After the Meeting

After the meeting, Daniel thinks optimistically about his chances and what type of service set-up would work best for PB Corporation. PB Corporation would need an outsourced CFO and basic accounting services, but he thinks it may not be a good idea to push this combination now, so he decides instead to focus on helping them where it hurts the most going forward. A typical outsourced CFO would cost around $3k-$4k/month, while standard accounting included would be at least double that. Daniel decides that once the CFO service is working, it will be easier for him to show how they could benefit from synergies combining his firm's CFO and accounting services, thereby positioning his company to replace the current accounting firm in the future.

Amanda has an internal meeting with Anders and also a short discussion with the finance manager, Peter, before her next call with Daniel. As Amanda and Daniel start their next call, she tells Daniel that PB Corp is very interested, but that it doesn't make sense to start working together until later next year. Anders doesn't think now is a good time to meet or pursue this opportunity with Daniel and his firm any further. Peter is equally negative as he thinks the changes going on in the business will make it difficult to shift how they currently handle PB Corporation's accounting and finances.

Peter's query, *"What if something goes wrong at such a crucial time?"* led to both Amanda and Anders having second thoughts.

Additionally, there is uncertainty in how fast the new bioplastics business will be able to scale up. Amanda says she still wants to hold the meeting with Daniel, as she thinks at least she'll get some good ideas by looking at the presentation and it will be easier for her to buy the needed help at a later point once she understands how the collaboration can be set-up.

"What next?" Daniel thinks to himself, as he evaluates whether he should spend more time with PB Corporation. The possibility of working together is now already pushed somewhere into the future.

Daniel tells Amanda that the outsourced CFO that he had in mind for the next meeting is very experienced in working with management teams of manufacturing companies of PB Corporation's size. They had actually already discussed that they were going to share some insights and ideas about the specific challenges PB Corporation is going to face. If Anders doesn't come to the meeting, then Daniel cannot, *"internally justify using a highly paid expert to join the meeting,"* Daniel explains. Daniel says it's okay for Anders to join the beginning of the meeting and then leave. Amanda seems to agree that Daniel's justification makes sense and she promises she will again try to get Anders to attend the meeting.

Within a few days Amanda confirms with Daniel that she has now succeeded at getting Anders to join the meeting. Without the first successful initial meeting, Daniel knows that Amanda would not be willing to go through this effort to repeatedly engage with the CEO to get him to attend. She trusts that it will be a worth-while meeting, based on the first meeting she had with Daniel, and now the next meeting should be even better since Daniel will be bringing another expert to share insights.

Meeting Checklists

Pre-meeting tasks	Yes	No
There is an agenda and a goal for the meeting		
You have sent the agenda to the attendees the day before the meeting		
You have set clear goals for what you want to achieve in the meeting		
You know if you will be creating demand or capturing demand (so you know what kind of selling situation you are in. You need to know if you need to challenge or consult the customer or compete with other vendors)		
You've researched the backgrounds and areas of responsibility of the people who you will be meeting		
You understand how each attendee fits into the company's overall organization chart		
You've done a background check on the prospects business and see whether it is growing or shrinking and how they've performed from a revenue and profit perspective.		
You have prepared material in advance if material is needed in the meeting		

Opening the Meeting	Yes	No
You start the meeting with the goal, agenda and time allotted to set the right expectations		
You allow for introductions of all meeting attendees and briefly talk about your company references and the results you can achieve (that's how you earn the right to ask questions)		
Open with a presentation that has relevant insights and statistics (as needed, especially in a situation where you need to create		

demand)		

Discovery: You are given, or are able to glean, the information you need on relevant topics, such as:	**Yes**	**No**
How is the market developing? Growing or shrinking?		
How are they doing? Relative to the market, are they growing or shrinking?		
What are their goals and objectives?		
What are their top priorities at the moment?		
How are they measuring success in these top priorities?		
What are the personal goals of the person you are meeting in relation to his/her role in the company?		
Do you know what stands in the way of the prospect achieving their goals?		
What are the reasons for their challenges?		
What have they already done to solve their problems?		
What are their other options for solving the problems? (as other competitors or current vendors can offer the product or service that are similar)		

Summarizing the discussion	**Yes**	**No**
You verbally summarize their goals and challenges and the customer can then confirm (verbally) that you have understood the key points of the discussion correctly		
You get verbal confirmation from the customer about what happens if their problems are not solved (Example: Can they live with the problem or is there a reason for fixing the problem sooner, rather than later?)		

	Yes	No
Is there a compelling business case for purchasing your solution right now or within a defined time-frame?		
Can you put a price on the risk that the customer takes if they do not make a decision?		
You discuss the different options of how the customer's problems can be solved (pros and cons)		

Next steps and qualification	Yes	No
Timeline for decision-making identified		
Decision-maker (the person who signs the contract) and decision-making process identified		
Budget/financing requirements identified		
Create a preliminary mutual timeline with the customer about the next steps that need to happen		
The customer shows commitment to moving forward together by dedicating their time and/or resources towards the defined next steps		

Post-meeting tasks	Yes	No
Memo of key points and next steps sent to customer		
Calendar invite with agenda sent to customer for next meeting		
LinkedIn invite sent after meeting (if not already sent in advance)		

Chapter 3: Creating Proposals

1 Booking meetings | 2 Running meetings | 3 Creating proposals | 4 Presenting | 5 Negotiating

Typical Challenges When Creating Proposals

Too product or service focused. Many proposal presentations have too many slides about the service or product features and not enough information about the customer's situation, challenges and outcomes they need to achieve. This leads to generic presentations that don't connect customer goals to the solutions you are selling. Oftentimes, the less a sales person truly understands a customer's goals and challenges, the more they try to explain their own products and services in hopes of saying something the customer will like. This approach leads to failure. Knowing your customer well is the best way to increase your chances of succeeding.

Sending or presenting a proposal too early. A salesperson often creates and sends a proposal to a customer who is not ready to buy. The customer's situation hasn't been properly appraised and the value that can be created has not yet been identified.

Not logically built from the buyer's perspective. The proposal presentation is often not organized logically, or, based on the client's needs. A proposal must start with the customer and lead towards the solution, not the other way around! Many sales professionals present the solution in the material without communicating the buyers specific pain points that will be solved so they can reach their goals & objectives. Additionally, as a buyer you want to compare the value you are getting with the investment. Many proposals lack a clear way for quantifying if the purchase makes financial sense for the buyer.

Creating and presenting the proposal to the wrong people. Presenting to the wrong people yet believing they can somehow make a purchase decision, or hoping that they are a strong internal influencer, is a big risk. In these cases, the sales person often relies too much on their one internal contact; the proposal that is created does not stand on its own when presented to others inside the company.

Without being able to talk to decision-makers and important influencers in the beginning of the sales process, it is next to impossible to craft a viable proposal.

Analyzing the Situation

It is October 9th. Daniel sits down at his office and begins by taking a moment to diagnose PB Corporation's situation on a high-level. He goes through all his notes and creates a mind-map on a piece of paper to focus on the most important topics from his discussion with Amanda. In the middle of the paper he writes PB Corporations most important goals, and around that middle he sketches in what things they must do to achieve the goals and what their potential risk and problems are. Afterwards, Daniel also internally discusses the case with his colleague Jim, a senior consultant, who Daniel was planning on bringing along to next meeting. Daniel also checks which one or two of their references would be the best fit for what PB Corporation's situation and goals are.

Daniel feels there is a huge risk that PB Corporation recognizes the need to buy, but still won't recognize a compelling enough reason to buy right now. In anticipation of this response, Daniel wants to build into the proposal a prediction of what will happen if they don't change. He will present one or two scenarios of what could happen, backed up by research and the insights of RFA's experienced CFO, that will help the client think about the risk of not acting on Daniel's proposal.

Creating the Proposal

Daniel takes a look at his previous proposal and creates a copy of it, saving it on his desktop as *PBCorp_version1*. He removes the old text and leaves the titles on the slides. He's going to use the same structure as the last presentation which had the following slides:

- Executive Summary
- Goals
- Challenges
- Options for solving Challenges
- The Solution
- References
- Benefits & Investment
- Project Timeline
- Next Steps

To get started, Daniel creates a mind-map like the one here below:

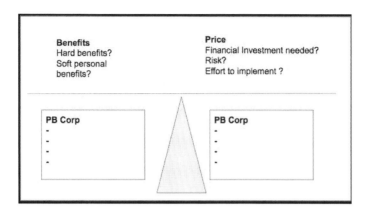

Daniel starts writing down what the most valuable benefits of what having an outsourced CFO are to PB Corp. He also wants to be realistic about the investment, not just from the perspective of what the costs of an outsourced CFO are, but also the cost of ramping up the new partnership. This exercise usually helps Daniel get started with creating a simple and powerful proposal.

Daniel knows that the better he can connect his offering to PB Corporation's strategic objectives, the easier it will be for them to see the value that RFA can provide. Daniel always tries to go one level above what the buyer is expecting of him and bring new points of view, so he becomes their trusted advisor or business partner, instead of just a person selling CFO- and accounting-services.

> *"89% of B2B buyers state that the vendors they've successful purchased from provided content that made it easier to show ROI and/or build a business case for the purchase."*[10]

Since PB Corporation said that they do not want to start anything new this year, Daniel and Jim, decide on building a proposal with a light ramp-up phase which starts at the end of this year already. The outsourced CFO will cost $30k annually with the set-up they are proposing, but with a two-year deal, its $55k—incentivizing the customer to spend more for a longer duration by offering upfront, long-term savings. Additionally, there will be a one-time service initiation fee of $10k, which will be done in December. Without the initiation fee, Daniel's firm cannot get started. While no further costs will be incurred until the following year, the $10k is something that Daniel knows may be an excuse for the customer to not sign the contract. But the service fee functions as a necessary guarantee of the customer's commitment and will not be an issue if a sales professional can tap into a customer's deep need/desire for change to facilitate future growth while simultaneously avoiding future pain.

At this point Daniel also knows he will need to put in a lot of effort to win a relatively small deal, but he sees potential with PB Corporation. The direction PB Corporation is heading as a company, as well as the new technology that RFA is developing, offer many different ways to grow PB Corporation into a strategic partner in the future.

Daniel decides that he will use reference cases to get the customer to commit in a light way, and then ramp up the opportunities to collaborate after three months. The first two months, December and January, will be light; starting in February of next year, RFA will be fully up and running with the outsourced CFO service. Typically, the collaboration starts with an audit, allowing the outsourced CFO to get to know the ins and outs of the business before taking on the standard responsibilities.

Simulating the Presentation

In order to make sure the meeting is successful, Daniel wants to coordinate how the material will be presented and how the different attendees will be engaged during the presentation. Daniel arranges an internal meeting with Jim, who will be joining him in the meeting. Jim will be the person to take over as PB Corporation's outsourced CFO if they get the deal. Daniel and Jim walk through the presentation and divide up the different tasks. Daniel will be responsible for opening the meeting and going through the executive summary, while Jim will then focus on specifics of the CFO service and how it will help solve PB Corporation's existing and future challenges. They also decide how they want to engage with Anders and on which specific parts of the presentation they want his feedback on. Daniel and Jim carefully choose what the key points are on each slide that require agreement from both Anders and Amanda before moving forward in the proposal.

Proposal Checklist

Tasks	Yes	No
The proposal is written from the customer's perspective, not from yours		
The proposal is logical and easy to understand		
If you are answering an RFP (request for proposal), you have had a chance to meet the customer and ask questions before creating the proposal		
The proposal has an executive summary in the beginning with a brief overall description of the discussions thus far, as well as a summary of the proposal content		
The customer's strategy, goals and pain points/challenges are documented in the proposal		
There is a clear business case or ROI calculation to help the customer choose your solution from a logical standpoint		
There is a clear connection between the solution and how the customer's problems will be solved and how their goals will be reached		
You've taken into account the buyer's different options and positioned yourself to win		
The customer's terminology has been used in the presentation		
There are suitable references in the proposal with examples of how you have helped others in similar situations		
Your solution and process are described in a simple way (use attachments for more detailed solution descriptions; this is not critical for decision-making but helpful nonetheless)		
There is an investment/price and benefits slide (preferably on the same page)		
There is a clear plan with a timeline and next steps		

Chapter 4: Presenting Proposals

Typical Challenges When Presenting Proposals

Forgetting that the presentation is just a communications tool. A proposal is just a tool to help you communicate better with the buyer (and the different stakeholders on the buyers' side), providing opportunities for insightful conversations about their objectives and challenges. This gives sales professionals the chance to understand the customer's situation better. When you have a true dialogue throughout the presentation, you won't lose focus. Sometimes, salespeople rush through their proposal and ask for the sale without knowing if the customer agrees with what has been shown to them.

Not leveraging a presentation to reach other stakeholders. Many salespeople don't gain access to key stakeholders in the beginning of the sales process. Presentations can be used as leverage points to get those tough-to-reach stakeholders included in meetings at a later point. Instead, many salespeople may accept a contact's word that they are in charge rather than pushing for key decision-makers who sign the contract to attend future meetings. Sales professionals need to push for contact with decision-makers to avoid becoming vulnerable to a single contact who may or may not be able to sell your ideas to others.

Not getting them to accept the solution, before introducing price. Many professionals can forget that presenting a solution is a dialogue that may be used to obtain confirmation on the buyer's challenges. A proposal presentation should never be used for telling the buyer what is already on the slides. When you gain consensus on each slide from the different participants and ensure that the solution is the right fit, you can then move on to topics like pricing and terms. Price is not relevant until the customer wants to buy something.

Presenting the Findings and the Solution

It's October 13th. Before the next meeting, Daniel sends along the agenda and the overall goal in a short e-mail to the stakeholders involved. He also scrolls through the presentation one more time to get a sense of the flow of the slides to ensure that everything is in a logical sequence. He also takes another look at the *PlastiTech Magazine* article; Daniel wants to refer to something from there to build rapport again with Anders. He quickly chooses which part of the article he will refer to during the meeting as he already remembers the different details outlined in it.

It's October 14th, the date of the second meeting. Daniel has only spoken to Anders on the phone and he seemed a little bit of grumpy. Anders has also expressed his opinion about not needing Daniel's services. Daniel knows that he needs to start the meeting off right and build rapport with Anders now that he will meet with him face to face, First-time meetings with key stakeholders are critical to the success of the sale.

In the beginning of the meeting, Daniel brings up a few things from the article as planned, and based on that, asks Anders if the year has gone as they have planned. Daniel further states that this is an interesting time in PB Corporation's history to be sitting down together, given the transformation ahead, and all the challenges therein. Daniel tries to not be overly excited or overly nice to Anders, instead, he is sincere, interested, attentive, polite, and very professional. Daniel has noticed that many executives can interpret this as kissing up to them— overplaying your hand with sycophantic responses will not help make the sale. You look desperate when you try too hard and Daniel wants to appear confident, capable of executing the solutions he is presenting to PB Corporation's key stakeholders.

After the small-talk and introductions at the beginning of the meeting, Daniel proceeds by stating the goal of the meeting, walking through the agenda to make sure it's okay with all the participants. The agenda allows Daniel to take participant's through the presentation at his own pace, including an executive summary as well as a deeper dive into PB Corporation's main objectives and challenges. After this, Daniel can delve into how the proposed solution solves PB Corporation's challenges and how RFA is uniquely qualified to provide that very solution.

Daniel states out loud that the primary goal is to ensure there is a good fit between PB Corporation's needs and what RFA can offer. If it is a good fit, then they will decide next steps for moving forward at the end of this meeting.

"Does that sound fair?" Daniel asks. They all agree that this is a good goal.

Daniel shows the first slide; the executive summary helps to facilitate a strategic discussion about the future plans of PB Corporation, which has been communicated both through the article that Daniel has read as well as the previous discussions with Amanda.

With every point that is on each slide, Daniel, or Jim, make sure that they get a confirmation from both Anders and Amanda. Now, in this particular meeting, Daniel is more aware of the need to get buy-in and engagement from Anders because Daniel knows that Anders is the key person who could stop this collaboration in its tracks. Anders has already made a statement about it not being the right time to proceed with RFA.

Daniel doesn't just want to present the findings and ask for the sale at the end of the presentation. Instead, Daniel wants the whole presentation to be a discussion towards agreement on key points by the key stakeholders, Amanda and Anders. Daniel doesn't just want a head nod; he wants proof that they agree and understand. And, if they do not agree, Daniel then hopes to discuss what they disagree on and why. Daniel wants an open and honest discussion. Asking, "Does that make sense?" is not enough of a pertinent question at the end of a slide for Daniel. Before moving on, he wants to make sure that the proper level of engagement is achieved, so he makes changes to the presentation as they speak to ensure both Anders's and Amanda's comments and their thoughts are included. On some points, Amanda wants a more detailed explanation, and on others, she asks that the language be changed as the terms didn't quite match PB Corporation's terminology. Daniel can sense full engagement from her. The presentation starts to become both of theirs, not just Daniel's. This is the way Daniel makes sure that this presentation is not about him and RFA's solutions but instead about the customer and their needs, and how he and RFA can meet those needs for the client. Daniel has noticed that the presentation needs to be very customer-oriented to achieve full engagement. If the client can clearly see themselves and their challenges in the presentation, then they will be more likely to want to correct & adjust what is written in the presentation.

Daniel, Jim, Amanda, and Anders move forward in the presentation once everything from the executive summary is covered, then shifting over to the slides with the objectives and the challenges of PB Corporation. Daniel also has a few key points on the challenges-slide about what the negative impact could be if the problems are not solved. He wants Anders and Amanda to clearly see what could happen next year if they do not agree to collaborate with RFA immediately. For example, "Profits could be severely impacted by about $2-million if procurement of new materials is not planned more efficiently than the current product line." Without his years of experience in the business and support from experts within RFA, Daniel would never be able to challenge the customers with such data, so he has learned to use internal knowledge and expertise wisely for the right cases and in the right situations. This is where Jim's support is crucial to Daniel, because without his expertise, it would be tough to challenge the customer.

Daniel's goal is to get Anders and Amanda to see what the risks are as they begin trying to scale up without fixing their current issues in how to track their financial performance.

On each slide, once there is agreement on the changes and modifications, the group moves on. By the time they reach the solution slide, there is a clear and logical path towards PB Corporation needing to do something about their challenges. Daniel would not have moved to the solution proposal slides if they didn't agree on the previous points regarding their goals & challenges leading up to the solution.

Instead of explaining the details of the outsourced CFO service and what it includes, Daniel explains what a typical outcome of this type of collaboration is, elegantly incorporating a reference story of one similar company in the manufacturing industry that experienced great success thanks to RFA. Daniel then lets Jim explain a few of the highlights of the service itself.

Through the discussion, Daniel gets several verbal confirmations that both Anders and Amanda see the value and feel the need to start collaborating, but the question is more about when the correct time to do it is.

Can they start immediately, or will the decision be put off until later in the spring next year, Daniel thinks to himself.

Daniel knows that if they postpone the decision until next year, there is always a risk that something else will happen and priorities could change, or, a competitor could enter the picture. From Daniel's perspective, he wants to make this deal move forward right now. It's not just in Daniel's best interest; he knows the customer is at risk if they do not make a decision about this before they are in even deeper trouble.

Daniel asks Anders and Amanda when they would like to start to see the results of the improved financial planning and visibility into their growing business; it's hard for the stakeholders to deny that they would like to see progress happen sooner rather than later. Daniel needs to give a realistic picture of what starting up the collaboration would mean and how fast it would be possible to initiate. He knows that if they started working together immediately, then PB Corporation would start seeing the benefits in Q1 of next year—that way PB

Corporation can also avoid the large potential risk of profit losses. Once Anders and Amanda understand this, then Daniel also shows a timeline on a slide so that he can get further commitment on next steps from them.

Daniel explains: *"These are the things that need to happen in order for us to reach the results by mid of Q1 so around February."*

Daniel walks them through a slide at the end of the presentation that shows a timeline with assumed dates and question marks. With the proposed timeline, they are able to backtrack from February and the results they want to achieve, all the way back to this day, October 14th.

Task	Timeline
Proposal	October 14th
Contract draft	?
Final agreement signed	?
Kick-off	November 21st
Onboarding CFO	December 5th
Full service in use	January 1st
Financial visibility achieved	February 15th

When looking at the timeline, Anders says it makes sense, but whether they want to start working together "*depends on the price.*"

"*Okay, let's move see what this type of set-up for you means from an investment perspective,*" Daniel says.

When Daniel moves to the next slide, he first shows the summarized goals and objectives that will be reached through the cooperation. He then shows the investment slide and shuts up. He does this so the customer fully understands the value versus the price, instead of just showing the price. This makes it easier for the customer to grasp that it makes sense to pay for the value he can provide. He shows the slide and doesn't say a word. He lets the complete picture sink in for the customer.

Daniel now wants to get an understanding of their true decision-making timeline and what must happen for PB Corporation stakeholders to move forward. After a moment of silence, Amanda says it all makes sense. Anders jumps in, suggesting he and Amanda consult with Peter, the finance manager, before making a final decision. A decision is made that a new meeting is needed where Amanda and the finance manager, Peter, are present.

After the official part of the meeting is over, Anders leaves for his next meeting. Amanda walks with Daniel and Jim back to the lobby. Amanda explains how she can definitely see how RFA's solutions would benefit PB

Corporation and that she will do what it takes to get this collaboration up and running. She is now very worried about next year; if Amanda doesn't get help with running the company, from a financial standpoint, the company will not reach its objectives, putting everyone's job at risk, not to mention the company itself.

Daniel is caught off guard, because Amanda didn't show a commitment this strong during the meeting when Anders was present, or, in any of their earlier discussions. Yet, Amanda is now positioning herself as Daniel's so called, "champion." Based on what she is now telling Daniel and how she is saying it, it seems that Amanda is not only willing to give Daniel her time, but she will actively drive this case forward to a close without Daniel being present. In Daniel's experience, this is extremely important because he hasn't won many deals where there isn't at least one key stakeholder that is very involved and emotionally attached to a positive outcome.

Gaining Commitment from Other Stakeholders

Daniel then holds a meeting with the same agenda on October 24th. The only difference is that now Anders is not in attendance. Instead, it will be Amanda and, Peter, the finance manager, who will be present. Unfortunately, Jim, has a schedule conflict so Daniel will have to manage running this meeting without the CFO-expert by his side.

Before the next meeting, Daniel really puts a lot of thought into how he can engage and interact with Peter, the finance manager, in a way that doesn't position RFA as a competitor or as a risk to Peter either looking bad or losing his job.

In the beginning of the meeting, Daniel wants to make sure that he positions RFA and the CFO-service in a way that can help

Peter in his job, instead of competing against him. Daniel has a few questions for Peter that Daniel prepared in advance to get Peter's point of view. Daniel is also able to slightly adjust the material and his key points compared to last meeting, so that the reference case is of another finance manager at another manufacturing company, stating how the help of RFA has been groundbreaking for their success.

In this particular case, RFA has also been able to save time for the finance manager, who stresses the importance of the continued help RFA can provide by saying:

"They are more than a partner; our CFO from RFA is more like a team member who can always help with the toughest financial challenges we are facing."

Peter seems quite happy with the meeting as Daniel patiently listens to his concerns and questions. To Peter, this meeting was positioned as a way to get to know a potential partner. He is unaware at this point that Amanda is serious about getting started as soon as possible.

After this meeting, Daniel and Amanda have another chat in the lobby. She says she will, again, present the proposal to the management team in their next meeting in a few weeks. She will recommend to the management team that they move forward and enter into an agreement with RFA.

After their management team-meeting, Amanda calls Daniel with a happy tone, to tell him they've made a decision that they want to move forward. They agree during that call that they should start drafting the contract and look over the terms and other details more closely.

Presentation Checklist

Pre-presentation	Yes	No
Are the right people attending the presentation meeting, especially the decision-maker(s)?		
Do you know everyone that will attend the meeting? If not, research their backgrounds		
Do you know what the key parts of the presentation are that you want the customer's confirmation on?		
Do you have a goal for the presentation meeting and a plan for what needs to happen after the meeting?		
If the presentation material will be presented from within the customer's organization, you know who will be presenting it internally?		
Does the person who will present your proposal truly want your solution to be chosen? If not, make sure they are first 100% convinced before allowing them to present your solution		
During presentation		
You get acceptance on each part of the presentation before moving on		
You get comments and confirmation on the key topics and problems presented		
You get confirmation that the buyer believes the solution is right for them and is the best option		
The next steps are clear—you know what needs to happen to get the contract signed		

Chapter 5:
Negotiating

| 1 Booking meetings | 2 Running meetings | 3 Creating proposals | 4 Presenting | 5 Negotiating |

Typical Challenges in the Negotiation Stage

Forgetting to sell first and negotiate second. Before the customer wants to buy there is no need to negotiate. Really, there is only ever a need to negotiate if there is something you disagree on, like the price. Attempting to move the deal forward too early without the client having a solid understanding of the true value and impact of the solution and an understanding of the customer's decision-making process are also common mistakes. Introducing pricing and terms before the customer has understood the value and is ready to buy is very common, and it leads to lower win-rates.

Focusing too much on price. Buyers get sales people to focus on price, but in reality, there are many other things that impact their willingness to buy. Price is not always as crucial of an issue as the buyer may be signaling.

Drafting the Contract

It is November 22nd. Now that Amanda has confirmed that PB Corporation wants to start the collaboration, Daniel and Amanda need to start going through the details of the contract and terms. Daniel drafts a typical RFA contract template and makes all the necessary modifications to the service offering scope, terms and pricing that they've discussed so far, sending it over to Amanda.

> *"Successful negotiation is 80% preparation."[11]*

But a red flag comes up. Amanda calls Daniel and says Anders has changed his mind and will not sign the contract until he discusses it with the board (the owners). It's a bit of a surprise to Amanda, but not so much to Daniel because along the way there were signals that the owners, who only recently retired, are still in the background and want to be involved in decision-making. Although Anders said he had the power to make the final decision, it now seems as if Amanda and Anders are not communicating well. They say that they need a time out to talk with the retired CEO. Perhaps Peter has mentioned something about this to the owners… Amanda also tells Daniel that she thinks that price will be an issue with Anders as it hasn't been budgeted for and that unless Daniel can do something about the price then it might not be possible to move forward after all. She says this is what Anders told her and she also seems to be more in a hurry than normal due to her business responsibilities, and she cannot schedule a call with Daniel for the upcoming days to discuss next steps due to her busy schedule. Some strategic project is going on and she says she must prioritize that fully right now.

Until now, Daniel felt like he was in control. But with Amanda being so busy and throwing several surprises at him at once, Daniel feels out of balance. He can't seem to get Amanda to engage in the same way as before because he doesn't exactly know what to do next. Daniel also learns during the call that PB Corporation has been quoted for a similar service for half the price from their current accounting partner. The finance manager, Peter, has been talking to the current accounting firm. Daniel is used to these types of situations as he often competes against someone that offers a similar service, but usually they don't actually have the right capabilities, experience or results to show for their work, so he doesn't let it bother him. He knows the current accounting partner is also saying they can help them with the same things as RFA, because they are afraid of losing an important client.

Although price is something that the buyer sometimes directs, Daniel knows there are so many other things impacting the decision; he acknowledges their comments about price but doesn't make a big deal about it. Price is just one part of doing business.

> *"8% of buyers said price is the main driver of their decision to select a specific vendor."*[12]

Daniel is a bit unhappy because he has put so much time into modifying the contract; he thought Amanda really meant that PB Corporation was serious about moving forward and that Anders would be able to sign once the modifications were made. Now, PB Corp is bringing up the price issue again…it feels like they are taking three steps forward, then two steps back.

With regards to Amanda's comments about price, Daniel once again reminds himself of something that one of his previous managers taught him:

"It is the customer's duty as an employee to do their best to get the best price and terms as possible for the company they represent. It's nothing personal and many customers even consider the negotiation to be fun as you get to see how sales people squirm and give in on their requests for decreasing price to get the deal they've been working so hard for."

Daniel realizes he didn't properly go through the step-by-step with Amanda of what would need to happen in order for them to get the contract signed. He assumed a bit too much. The discussion he is now having with Amanda should have happened much earlier.

Daniel and Amanda end the call, deciding that Amanda will let Daniel know how discussions with the former CEO went.

Daniel decides he will not make any changes to his proposal or the contract that he had already sent, even though Amanda said it might be a good idea to make a few specific changes if Daniel wants the contract to be signed as soon as possible.

It takes several days for Amanda to get an answer back to Daniel, and she seems positive, but Anders is not yet willing to give his full support for this decision, because their current finance manager "has always been enough," which is what Anders said was relayed by the former CEO. What is interesting is that they are willing to make large investment decisions, but smaller ones like this one are difficult especially if unplanned and therefore not budgeted the previous fall.

Anders and Amanda seem to be in charge but somehow the former CEO's presence makes them ineffective at making decisions. It is starting to become clear to Daniel, that although Anders has been hired to run the company, the former CEO is still very much in charge.

Daniel proposes to Amanda that they need to approach this from a new angle with long-term thinking in order to make a proper presentation for the former CEO. They decide to put together a presentation that will start with PB Corporation's long-term strategy and targets; this will be created on PB Corporation's own presentation templates. Daniel proposes that Amanda presents the material to the former CEO, and not Anders.

Designing a Win-Win Situation

It's November 26th. Amanda and Daniel have an online meeting to create the new presentation.

Daniel wants to make the presentation for the former CEO and current owner about two things: First, highlight the risk of losing out on profits in the coming year, and second, to stress the risk of not reaping the benefits of their acquisition-investment. Profit and growth need to be managed and controlled— this is what the key to winning this deal is about.

Daniel and Amanda prepare the presentation and decide that Amanda, together with Anders, will present if for the former CEO in an extra meeting they will book immediately.

Since Amanda is his champion, Daniel wants to make sure she is the one that looks like the hero when PB Corporation makes the decision, so he coaches her on the presentation and the key points.

It's December 4th. Amanda calls Daniel after her meeting with Anders and the former CEO. It seems as if the new presentation and Amanda's commitment and desire to get

RFA as their partner has worked. They agree that they need the service Daniel has been proposing, but both Anders and the former CEO want Amanda to re-evaluate if they could get this service from the current accounting partner. The former CEO said he doesn't need to be involved anymore. He understands the situation better and even gave Amanda praise for her good work. Amanda tells Daniel that she wants to work with RFA and now she just needs a few improvements in the terms. She gives some pointers to Daniel on what she thinks are the exact things that need to be included in the updates of the contract so she can have Anders sign it. She wants some clarification in the terms so she can say that she not only compared the two different service providers but was also able to squeeze a better deal out of RFA.

Daniel holds an additional meeting with RFA's legal department to smooth out the few things in the contract that Amanda pointed out, which turn out to be very minor details. Daniel sends over the updated contract.

Finalizing and Signing

It's December 10th. Amanda calls Daniel. She starts the call by asking Daniel how he is, then adds, *"Listen Daniel, Anders was still tough on me…. but we can now go ahead and finally sign the agreement!"*

The contract is signed that afternoon electronically by Anders.

Daniel is almost a bit surprised because, in the end, everything went quite fast once he understood how to team up with Amanda and how to strategically position the proposed collaboration.

Starting the Delivery

At this point, Daniel wants to make sure RFA starts the work right away because there is always a risk of the customer cancelling their order if something negative happens in their business. The kick-off, and other necessary meetings, are booked immediately. The kick-off is scheduled on the 15th of December, almost right on target as planned earlier in the fall when they discussed the schedule for the first time.

By the end of January, Daniel sits down with Amanda to review how things have gone with Jim, the outsourced CFO from RFA. They also discuss how PB Corporation will continue to make investments in their business, including what new recruitments need to be made, at which point Amanda shares the news that the finance manager, Peter, will be retiring.

After the meeting, Daniel sits in his car and evaluates the changes going on at PB Corporation, all of which are new opportunities for future sales. Not only are there changes at PB Corporation, but RFA is also changing as they have just purchased a software consulting company. RFA's new acquisition focuses on software that could fit very nicely with PB Corporation's needs.

PB Corporation is poised to become a strong strategic partner for RFA moving forward. High-performance sales are about both growth and growth-potential. You're selling more than just a product or a service— you're also building bridges to mutually beneficial (and profitable!) partnerships.

Negotiation Checklist

Tasks	Yes	No
Before sending the contract, the buyer has confirmed that they want to buy your solution		
Do you know who you will be negotiating the terms with? In other words, will it be directly with the decision-maker, an influencer/decision making committee, or procurement?		
Do you understand the buyer's decision-making process?		
Do you have a "walk away line" for your price and terms?		
Have you been able to quantify the positive financial impact of your solution before entering negotiations? • This will be your biggest asset in the negotiation from a psychological and evidentiary stand-point		
Can you see a clear win-win for both parties • When tough conflicts with price and terms come up, have a problem-solving attitude--this doesn't mean you come down in price, it just means you need to have a cooperative, flexible and professional attitude		

Final Words

Although Daniel hit some speed bumps on his road to success, he was able to navigate through the problems because he was consistent and persevered. When he uncovered new problems, Daniel wasn't passive; instead, he actively looked for solutions to work around the problems. This type of problem-solving and forward-looking attitude will get you far in the sales profession.

Without a proper diagnosis of the customer's situation in the beginning of the sales process, it's impossible to build customer-centric proposals. You'll end up placing a lot of emphasis on closing the sale, often associated with different types of pressure-tactics used to bully buyers into making a quick decision they'll later regret. Even slightly more complex B2B buying decisions require the involvement of several stakeholders. You'll need a "yes" or "okay" from every stakeholder to get a win.

I work with many sales leaders that are worried about their sales people lacking "closing skills." When we start diagnosing why the sales reps are having a hard time "closing," it becomes very apparent that the way these sales people are discovering and diagnosing the customer's situations are really the problem, not their closing skills. When we examine a long buying process that is coming to its natural end, there isn't that much room for creativity or influencing the buying decision any longer. That's why closing shouldn't bear that much weight. Instead, focus on doing the right things in the beginning and everything else in later stages will be much easier.

The difference between winners and losers today is the quality of the discussions that sales people have with buyers early in the sales process.

> **"74% of buyers choose the sales rep that is first to add value and insight"**
> *(Corporate Visions)*

Daniel was able to get off to a good start because he was able to meet with the management first. If Daniel started by contacting the finance manager, there would never have been a deal. Having sales discussion skills doesn't matter if you aren't talking to the right people about the right subjects. It was the business leader, Amanda, who was ambitious enough to drive the needed change. This was crucial for Daniel's ability to quickly build and close a relatively complex sale within a few short months.

Daniel was also able to position himself early in the game as a trusted advisor. He did his research and got in at the right time, fostering a healthy relationship with stakeholders based on trust. This combination of his timing and his approach are what resulted in a great victory for Daniel.

Since Daniel was able to find some challenges and connect them to PB Corporation's goals, he was in a great position to consult on what was needed for success with their future goals. Since he had helped Amanda see their situation from new angles, she also felt emotionally connected, appreciative of Daniel's work. These are a few reasons why most deals go to the sales person that first provide added value and share relevant insights.

Compared to the story in this book, many more meetings would likely be needed in more complex B2B deals. In a real-life situation, the checklist for chapter two would be used in several different meetings. In Daniel's case, we skipped a separate discovery meeting since he was able to get enough information in the first meeting. Daniel did a good job of setting up his opportunity, then thinking about how to drive the opportunity to a close together with Amanda. The three things that were left out that are very typical as we move to more complex sales include dealing with legal departments, procurement, as well as RFPs. Sales professionals are facing legal and procurement more often than ever before.

By following the best practices provided by the checklists, it will be easier to face obstacles presented by legal and procurement departments, but I decided these would not be focused on in this book. Instead, we focused on getting the basics down so that you have the right foundation to succeed when sales become more complex.

Remember, the checklists are only as good as how you use them. The more professional you are as a sales person, the more capable you'll be of properly utilizing the checklists.

I advise you to practice, gaining as much experience through as many different situations as possible, reflecting on both your wins and losses. Each meeting and each call with a customer is a chance to get better at your craft, so make sure you make the most of every opportunity and keep learning.

Happy selling!

Templates & Tools

A handful of readers in the early stages of creating this book asked how the presentations and different templates that Daniel use could be shared. When thinking about the best way to share them, I reflected on the best coaches and mentors I've had and how those individuals have helped me implement effective strategies in my own work. There's no one-size-fits-all answer; it's not about teaching (or learning) one specific tool and method, but about deeply understanding why and how to use the tools you have.

For this reason, I decided to combine the tools of highly-effective professionals as well as the checklists that help them work smarter not harder, along with the proper coaching to use these strategies to their fullest potential. I have combined all these elements into a new online course.

By taking this course you will very quickly grasp the concepts and you'll get all the checklist and templates you'll need to succeed. This will accelerate how fast you can implement everything covered in the book.

Although traditional sales training can be effective, this online course takes a different approach. The course allows you to get what you need by implementing it on a daily basis, rather than cramming for a few days straight, like in traditional training.

The online course dives deeply into each of the five areas you need to master to be successful in sales. For each chapter, you'll get templates—for example, a prospecting template, email templates, 1st meeting presentation templates for creating demand and challenging customers, proposal templates, etc.

Sign up for the course at courses.janropponen.com to get access to the templates and training right away!

Sales Habits Workshop

To help sales managers speed up the learning process of their sales teams, I have created a method for sales people to diagnose what areas they need to focus on and improve their results in one workshop.

The Sales Habit Workshop is a good way for managers to get development ideas for their sales people and help them identify which specific methods need improvement or change, and, in which situations to implement that change. It's much more effective when sales professionals do their own diagnoses, rather than a manager telling them what's wrong and why.

In the workshop each sales person receives a score on each part of the five steps and they also create a development plan with specific action points.

The poster below is used in the workshop to analyze each part referenced in this volume, from booking meetings to negotiating deals. Be in touch if you are interested in doing the workshop together.

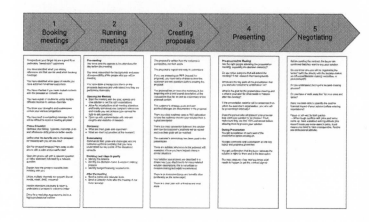

About the author

Jan Ropponen advises and trains both B2B sales management and sales executives on topics such as modern sales processes and methodologies, as well as opportunity management.

He works with companies from industries such as telecom, manufacturing, media, insurance and technology.

In previous roles Jan has worked both in management and sales positions in companies with services that cover CRM and marketing automation technologies, as well as digital marketing services.

Contact Jan via e-mail or visit his website:
Jan.ropponen@axend.fi
www.janropponen.com

About Daniel Masters*

Daniel is a 38-year-old sales professional, who started his sales career when he was 26 years old. Daniel works for an accounting and financial services firm called Ross Finance and Accounting,

Year after year he has been improving his results as an account manager and his goal is to become a CEO one day, although he still wants to keep selling for many more years.

If you are interested in hearing more about how Daniel sells, please write him a message to tell him what you would like to hear about next. I will write the next story based on the requests of readers.

Sending Daniel an e-mail: mastersdaniel439@gmail.com

*Disclaimer: Daniel is a fictional character; any resemblance to other people is purely coincidental. His purpose and reason for existence is to make learning about sales less boring and help sales people become more successful. (image: Freepik.com)

Summary of the checklists

Prospecting Checklists

Tasks	Yes	No
Prospects on your target list are a good fit or, preferably, "sweet-spot" customers for the products and services you provide		
You have identified what your strong references are that can be used when booking meetings		
You have identified what types of results you have achieved for similar customers before contacting the prospect		
You have checked if you have mutual contacts with the prospect on LinkedIn or connections in other social channels you can leverage		
You understand the changes and trends going on in the prospect's industry right now and how they impact the prospect's business		
You have information about changes going on within the prospect's company (these changes can be organizational changes, new products etc. which can act as triggers that open up a window of opportunity for new vendors and solutions)		
You have a plan or routine for using multiple different touches in various channels (email, phone, LinkedIn, SMS, voicemail etc.)		
You know your strengths and weaknesses versus your various competitors		
You have a compelling message and can leverage your unique value proposition in such a way that it will make it difficult to reject a meeting proposal		

If none of the above get you a meeting with your dream prospect, you have a way to follow the prospect and their business until a suitable event happens that will trigger them to want to meet with you		

Meeting Checklists

Pre-meeting tasks	Yes	No
There is an agenda and a goal for the meeting		
You have sent the agenda to the attendees the day before the meeting		
You have set clear goals for what you want to achieve in the meeting		
You know if you will be creating demand or capturing demand (so you know what kind of selling situation you are in. You need to know if you need to challenge or consult the customer or compete with other vendors)		
You've researched the backgrounds and areas of responsibility of the people who you will be meeting		
You understand how each attendee fits into the company's overall organization chart		
You've done a background check on the prospects business and see whether it is growing or shrinking and how they've performed from a revenue and profit perspective.		
You have prepared material in advance if material is needed in the meeting		

Opening the Meeting	Yes	No
You start the meeting with the goal, agenda and time allotted to set the right expectations		
You allow for introductions of all meeting attendees and briefly talk about your company references and the results you can		

achieve (that's how you earn the right to ask questions)		
Open with a presentation that has relevant insights and statistics (as needed, especially in a situation where you need to create demand)		

Discovery: You are given, or are able to glean, the information you need on relevant topics, such as:	**Yes**	**No**
How is the market developing? Growing or shrinking?		
How are they doing? Relative to the market, are they growing or shrinking?		
What are their goals and objectives?		
What are their top priorities at the moment?		
How are they measuring success in these top priorities?		
What are the personal goals of the person you are meeting in relation to his/her role in the company?		
Do you know what stands in the way of the prospect achieving their goals?		
What are the reasons for their challenges?		
What have they already done to solve their problems?		
What are their other options for solving the problems? (as other competitors or current vendors can offer the product or service that are similar)		

Summarizing the discussion	**Yes**	**No**
You verbally summarize their goals and challenges and the customer can then confirm (verbally) that you have understood the key points of the discussion correctly		

135

	Yes	No
You get verbal confirmation from the customer about what happens if their problems are not solved (Example: Can they live with the problem or is there a reason for fixing the problem sooner, rather than later?)		
Is there a compelling business case for purchasing your solution right now or within a defined time-frame?		
Can you put a price on the risk that the customer takes if they do not make a decision?		
You discuss the different options of how the customer's problems can be solved (pros and cons)		

Next steps and qualification	Yes	No
Timeline for decision-making identified		
Decision-maker (the person who signs the contract) and decision-making process identified		
Budget/financing requirements identified		
Create a preliminary mutual timeline with the customer about the next steps that need to happen		
The customer shows commitment to moving forward together by dedicating their time and/or resources towards the defined next steps		

Post-meeting tasks	Yes	No
Memo of key points and next steps sent to customer		
Calendar invite with agenda sent to customer for next meeting		
LinkedIn invite sent after meeting (if not already sent in advance)		

Proposal Checklist

Tasks	Yes	No
The proposal is written from the customer's perspective, not from yours		
The proposal is logical and easy to understand		
If you are answering an RFP (request for proposal), you have had a chance to meet the customer and ask questions before creating the proposal		
The proposal has an executive summary in the beginning with a brief overall description of the discussions thus far, as well as a summary of the proposal content		
The customer's strategy, goals and pain points/challenges are documented in the proposal		
There is a clear business case or ROI calculation to help the customer choose your solution from a logical standpoint		
There is a clear connection between the solution and how the customer's problems will be solved and how their goals will be reached		
You've taken into account the buyer's different options and positioned yourself to win		
The customer's terminology has been used in the presentation		
There are suitable references in the proposal with examples of how you have helped others in similar situations		
Your solution and process are described in a simple way (use attachments for more detailed solution descriptions; this is not critical for decision-making but helpful nonetheless)		
There is an investment/price and benefits slide (preferably on the same page)		

There is a clear plan with a timeline and next steps		

Presentation Checklist

Pre-presentation	Yes	No
Are the right people attending the presentation meeting, especially the decision-maker(s)?		
Do you know everyone that will attend the meeting? If not, research their backgrounds		
Do you know what the key parts of the presentation are that you want the customer's confirmation on?		
Do you have a goal for the presentation meeting and a plan for what needs to happen after the meeting?		
If the presentation material will be presented from within the customer's organization, you know who will be presenting it internally?		
Does the person who will present your proposal truly want your solution to be chosen? If not, make sure they are first 100% convinced before allowing them to present your solution		
During presentation		
You get acceptance on each part of the presentation before moving on		
You get comments and confirmation on the key topics and problems presented		
You get confirmation that the buyer believes the solution is right for them and is the best option		
The next steps are clear—you know what needs to happen to get the contract signed		

Negotiation Checklist

Tasks	Yes	No
Before sending the contract, the buyer has confirmed that they want to buy your solution		
Do you know who you will be negotiating the terms? In other words, will it be directly with the decision-maker, an influencer/decision making committee, or procurement?		
Do you understand the buyer's decision-making process?		
Do you have a "walk away line" for your price and terms?		
Have you been able to quantify the positive financial impact of your solution before entering negotiations? • This will be your biggest asset in the negotiation from a psychological and evidentiary stand-point		
Can you see a clear win-win for both parties • When tough conflicts with price and terms come up, have a problem-solving attitude--this doesn't mean you come down in price, it just means you need to have a cooperative, flexible and professional attitude		

Notes

1 - Salespeople Perceptions and Top Performance Study 2018, Marc Wayshak Communications LLC

2 - Sales Benchmark Index 2013
https://business.linkedin.com/content/dam/business/sales-solutions/global/en_US/c/pdfs/linkedin-sbi-sales-research-report-us-en-130920.pdf

3 - The Sales Development Technology Report
https://blog.topohq.com/sales-development-technology-the-stack-emerges/

4 - Hubspot Research,
https://blog.hubspot.com/sales/salespeople-perception-problem?_ga=2.41538218.989260216.1539615804-215345474.1536196549

5 - *Source: SiriusDecisions*

6 - Top Performance in Sales Prospecting Benchmark Report, RAIN Group (2018)

7 - *Hubspot Sales Perception Survey Q1, 2016*
https://research.hubspot.com/charts/what-buyers-want-to-talk-about-in-the-first-sales-call

8 - *Hubspot Sales Perception Survey Q1, 2016*
https://research.hubspot.com/charts/what-buyers-want-to-talk-about-in-the-first-sales-call

9 - Gartner Group

10 - *2017 B2B Buyer's survey report*
http://e61c88871f1fbaa6388d-c1e3bb10b0333d7ff7aa972d61f8c669.r29.cf1.rackcdn.com/DGR_DG061_SURV_B2B_Buyers_Jun_2017_Final.pdf

11 - Clive Rich, (2011) "Successful negotiation is 80 percent preparation: How to get more of what you want by preparing properly", Strategic Direction, Vol. 27 Issue: 3, pp.3-5, https://doi.org/10.1108/02580541111109543

12 - SiriusDecisions 2015 buying study https://www.siriusdecisions.com/blog/price notthemostimportantdriverofbtobbuyingdecisions

Made in the USA
Middletown, DE
14 August 2019